The eency weency spider

1.

went up the water spout.

2.

Down came the rain

and washed the spider out.

4.

Out came the sun.

5.

and dried up all the rain.

The eency weency spider

went up the spout again.

The Eency Weency Spider

D. F. SCHOTT EDUCATIONAL MATERIALS

Little Steps to Reading

Pasitos hacia la lectura

D. F. SCHOTT EDUCATIONAL MATERIALS
P. O. BOX 5296
VENTURA, CA 93005
(805) 646-8508

ISBN: 1-56537-070-8

The eency weency spider

1.

went up the spout again.

8.

went up the water spout.

2.

The eency weency spider

7.

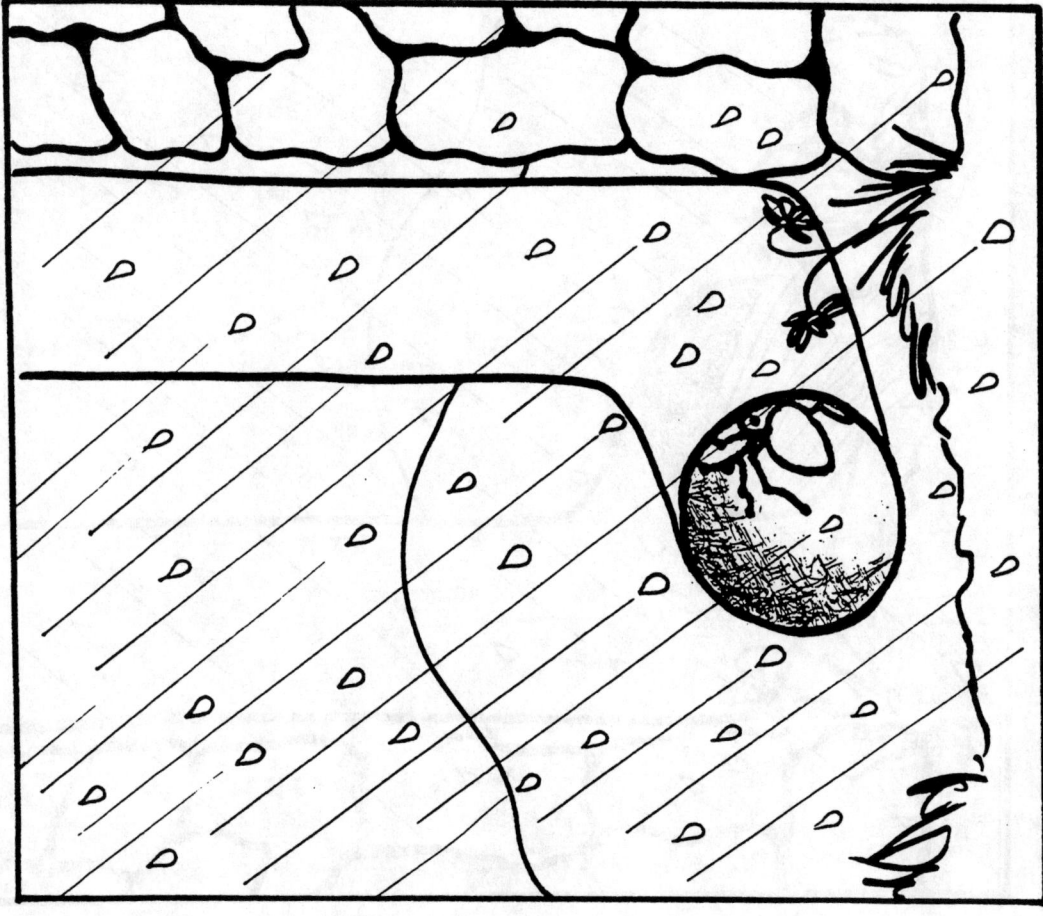

Down came the rain

3.

and dried up all the rain.

6.

and washed the spider out.

4.

Out came the sun.

5.